T0095346

JUST A
CLOSER WALK

JUST A CLOSER WALK

Jonathan Temple

WESTBOW®
PRESS
A DIVISION OF THOMAS NELSON
& ZONDERVAN

WestBow Press books may be ordered through booksellers or by contacting:

WestBow Press
A Division of Thomas Nelson & Zondervan
1663 Liberty Drive
Bloomington, IN 47403
www.westbowpress.com
1 (866) 928-1240

Edited by Dr. Frank Battles and Sonja Myers

Special Thanks to Jim LaRussa for all the help and encouragement finalizing, Just a Closer Walk.

ISBN: 978-1-4908-6672-7 (sc)
ISBN: 978-1-4908-6671-0 (e)

Library of Congress Control Number: 2015902368

Print information available on the last page.

WestBow Press rev. date: 4/21/2015

Dedication

To my beautiful wife Lisa,
Thank you for always believing in me.

Foreword

~

Just A Closer Walk is a 31-day devotional book inspired by a realization that it is God who desires a closer walk with us. The Great I Am, The Alpha and Omega, The Lover of Our Soul, our Salvation; the list could go on. It is God who is chasing us. It is God who wants to spend time with us, more than we realize. God truly loves us. We do not have to earn His love. We do not have to work our spiritual fingers to the bone to earn His love or favor. Through Jesus our Savior, we have God's total love, grace, and mercy. He did not send Jesus to die on the cross for us so He could have an army of worker bees or an army of "yes men" or a people who are just plain scared of going to Hell. Through the ages, God has always reached out to people and to the world. God didn't go to all the trouble of sending Jesus, his Son, merely to point a condemning finger so that we all walk around feeling bad about ourselves. God sent Jesus to show us how a loving and merciful He is. A young man was once asked by his friends how he knew he was saved. The young man thought for a while, and then said, "You know how it is when you go fishing and catch a fish? You can't see the fish, you only feel it tugging on the line. That's how it was when I got saved. I just felt God tugging on my heart". My hope as you read and interact with these daily devotions for the next 31 days is that God will tug on your heart in a gentle, loving way, and that you will realize just how much you are loved and cherished by your Heavenly Father.

I wrote many of these devotionals for my church bulletin. I thank my pastor, Dr. Frank Battles, for allowing me the freedom to contribute to the church bulletin and for his help in the editing process. Many of these devotionals are ones I have shared while on mission trips in Central and South America. I owe a great deal of thanks to my father, Jack Temple, Sr., for giving me the chance to share on those mission trips. Thanks Dad! These devotionals are written from the heart, many times out of the daily struggles I have faced and sometimes still face. I am a regular person, just like everyone else; I have had, and still face, the daily struggles of life. I have come to realize that I am just the sort of person God uses to illustrate His great love, mercy, and forgiveness. I have at times been broken and wounded, sometimes by my own bad choices. God, with His great love and mercy, has never and will ever give up on me! I want to show others not to give up when they make mistakes or come up short. No matter what you have or have not done, no matter how far you think you have wandered away from God, I want you to know that God still loves you. His arms are open to receive you back into fellowship with Him and to experience a walk with Him. I want you to know that God is chasing you and wants to be a part of your daily life. Let the adventure begin, for you are loved more than you could ever know!

Just A Closer Walk

How *Just A Closer Walk* is set up

Just A Closer Walk is a 31-day devotional journey. It can start on any day you choose, or you can wait until the first day of the month to start.

As you open the book, you will notice there are two pages for each day. Each day is numbered and begins on the left side with the devotional for that day.

The second page, the right side of the book, is titled **Today's Closer Walk,** which begins with a scripture or scriptures that support the theme of that day's devotional.

Next is **Down the Path,** which is separated into two parts: **Sure Footing** and **Solid Ground. Sure Footing** is designed to guide the reader and suggest what he or she may need to understand from the reading.

Solid Ground is a suggested response or reaction to the devotional. **Solid Ground** is designed to build the faith of the reader through the day's theme. It is a way to put that day's devotion into action.

Talking with Jesus is a short, specific prayer to ask God for help and strength to walk out that day's devotion.

Let the journey begin!

DAY 01

A Closer Walk

"Just a closer walk with Thee, Grant it, Jesus, is my plea, Daily walking close to Thee, Let it be, dear Lord, let it be." It is an old song, but it is always new and refreshing to me. This continues to be my anthem as I walk with Jesus. Many times I sing this song driving down the road or in my alone time with the Lord. One day, I heard this song in a different way. It wasn't me singing to the Lord, He was singing to me. I did not hear an audible voice. It was that still, small, quiet, gentle voice of the Good Shepherd. God is always reaching out to us. He desires fellowship with us, his children. He desires to be a part of our lives, not in a casual way, but in a deep personal relationship. Here is what I heard: **"Just a closer walk with thee, Grant it, child, is my plea, daily walking close to thee, let it be dear child, let it be."** As I heard these words, my spirit soared and I began to sing, "Yes Lord, Yes, to your will and to your way, when your Spirit speaks to me with my whole heart I'll agree and my answer will be, yes Lord, Yes!" Jesus said in Revelations 3:27: "Behold, I stand at the door and knock; if anyone hears My voice and opens the door, I will come in to him and will dine with him, and he with Me" (NIV). It is not just in the moment of salvation that Jesus knocks, but in every area of our lives. Jesus stands at our hearts' door in an earnest desire to fellowship with us. His plea is to fellowship with His children. He wants us, not by force or by fear, but through our willingness to be drawn to Him by His deep, unfailing love for us. James 4:7 says, "Come close to God and He will come close to you" (NIV). It is by our invitation that the Lord takes part in our lives. **"Just a closer walk with thee, Grant it child is my plea, daily walking close to thee, Let it be dear child. Let it be."** Will your answer be "Yes Lord, Yes"?

Today's Closer Walk

I have no greater joy than to hear that my children walk in truth. 3 John 1:4

If we live in the Spirit, let us also walk in the Spirit. Galatians 5:25

The path of the righteous is level; O upright One, you make the way of the righteous smooth. Isaiah 26:7

Thou hast enlarged my steps under me; so that my feet did not slip. 2 Samuel 22:37

Down the Path

Sure Footing

Let it be dear child, let it be. God wants to fellowship with you; He wants to be a part of your life every day in a unique and special way. God wants to fellowship with you far more than He wants you to do works for Him.

Solid Ground

Say yes to God's desire to fellowship with you. Jesus says in Revelation 3:20,

"Look at me. I stand at the door. I knock. If you hear me call and open the door, I'll come right in and sit down to supper with you." (The Message)

Talking with Jesus

Prayer

Lord Jesus, I say yes to Your desire to want to be a part of my life. Not just the big parts, but even the insignificant everyday parts. I open my heart's door to a closer walk with You. I thank You that You and I will walk closer today! Amen.

What are your thoughts as you choose a closer walk with Jesus?

JUST FOR THE CHANCE

"Step right up folks, three chances for a dollar! Win the biggest teddy bear in the world, three chances for a dollar!" The carnival barker was trying to get the attention of the people passing by. "Three chances for a dollar" to win the "biggest teddy bear in the world," would be a small investment for a great opportunity to impress someone important. *Chance:* some define it as luck. One dictionary defines it as the possibility or probability that something will happen. I am no theologian, but I believe that one day Jesus took a chance on me...and you!

"For God so loved the world that He gave His only Son. Whoever puts his trust in God's Son will not be lost but will have life that lasts forever" (NIV, John 3:16). Jesus was born into a world out of touch with God. There was no other way that mankind could experience the love of the True and Living God. He walked among ordinary people. He taught them. He revealed the way of true love. He taught through word and deed of God's everlasting, unconditional love. Jesus broke religious traditions in order to touch those who needed God the most. He said, "God's Spirit is on me; He's chosen me to preach the Message of Good News to the poor, sent me to announce pardon to prisoners and recovery of sight to the blind, To set the burdened and battered free" (The Message, Luke 4:18). Jesus fulfilled God's plan to bridge the gap between man and God, to bring salvation and fellowship with God to a lost world. He was innocent, but still He was crucified. He was buried in a borrowed tomb. He rose from the dead. He ascended to heaven to the right hand of God as our Intercessor. Jesus, our Savior, chose to make this incredible journey **just for the chance to fellowship with us,** *now,* in this life, and *forever,* in eternity. How incredible it is that Jesus took a chance on us. He left the splendor of heaven so that we might experience the love of the Father. He lived so that through him we would have an opportunity to know God. **He lived for the chance to know us.** There was no guarantee the world would accept Him. In fact, John 1:11 tells us, "He came to his own people, but they didn't want him" (NIV). Jesus is called the stone that the builders rejected. The religious leaders who were supposed to recognize their Messiah cast Jesus away like a builder would cast away an odd-shaped stone that was unfit for use. Through love and the desire to please the Father, Jesus came into the world as a sacrifice to clear away our sins and guilt so that we could know Him. This is the kind of love we are talking about—not that we once upon a time loved God, but that he loved us and sent his Son as a sacrifice to clear away our sins and the damage they've done to our relationship with God. 1 John 4:10 says, "Not that we loved God, But that He loved us" (NIV). We have the power of loving Him, because He first revealed and demonstrated His love for us. Jesus made an inconceivable journey just for the chance to know us. He did this by loving us first. Let our Lord and Savior show you how much He loves you, for He lived and died... *just for the chance.*

Today's Closer Walk

Scripture(s)

Come to me, all you who are weary and burdened, and I will give you rest.
Matthew 11:28

Down the Path

Sure Footing

Jesus took a chance so that one day He would be able to fellowship with you! He broke with the traditional religious thinking of his day to show you how much He loves and cares for you: Jesus wants to walk with you today! Fellowship with Him today.

Solid Ground

Let Jesus love you! He made an incredible journey and sacrifice so that you would not be lost and alone. Let Jesus love you. He lived, died, and rose from the dead just for the chance to love and know you.

Talking with Jesus

Prayer

Lord Jesus, thank You for Your life, death, and resurrection. I accept Your call to fellowship with me. Let's walk together today. Amen.

What are your thoughts as you choose a closer walk with Jesus?

THE FOG AND THE SHORE

In 1952, Florence Chadwick, a world-class distance swimmer, attempted to swim the chilly ocean waters between Catalina Island and the California shore. This was Florence's first attempt at such a monumental task. Florence swam through foggy weather and choppy seas for fifteen hours. Her muscles began to cramp, and her resolve weakened. She begged to be taken out of the water, but her mother, riding in a boat alongside, urged her not to give up. She kept trying, but she grew exhausted and stopped swimming. Aids lifted her out of the water and into the boat. They paddled a few more minutes, the mist broke, and she discovered that the shore was less than a half-mile away. "All I could see was the fog," she explained at a news conference, "I think if I could have seen the shore, I would have made it."

In our faith journey we often focus on our circumstances and where we are at the moment instead of what God has promised and the goals He has placed in our hearts. It is easy to focus on the fog created by what we are going through. The fog creates more questions of doubt than it affirms answers of faith. We wonder how the bills will get paid. We wonder if our life is on the right path. We wonder if we will realize the dreams that fill our hearts. There is no end to the doubtful questions when we focus on what we cannot see. Florence Chadwick focused on the fog. The fog created questions. "How far is the shore? It can't be close, because I don't see it." The fog Florence saw masked the reality of where she was in her journey. The shore was closer than Florence realized. She said, "If I could have seen the shore, I would have made it."

Your shore is closer than you think! The achievement of your goal takes one step at a time and each step you take brings you closer to reaching the shore! Do not let the fog get in the way of seeing God's plan for your life. Don't let the fog steal your victory. Keep going, continue to believe, and hang on to what you have asked for. Don't let go of your dreams.

In Luke 18:1, Jesus told a parable to the effect that we ought to always pray and not turn coward (NIV). Hebrews 11 tells us, "Trust in God is the firm foundation under everything that makes life worth living. **It's our handle on what we can't see"** (NIV, Hebrews 11:1).

Florence made another attempt at swimming from Catalina Island to Palos Verdes, CA. In 1952, Florence Chadwick swam the 21 miles from Catalina

Island to Palos Verdes in 13 hours, 47 minutes, and 32 seconds, breaking a record that had been set in 1927. In August 8, 1950, when she crossed the English Channel in 13 hours and 20 minutes, she broke the world record held by American swimmer Gertrude Ederle. One year later, Chadwick crossed the English Channel yet again, from England to France; this time, in 16 hours and 22 minutes, thus making her the first woman to swim the English Channel in both directions. This time the fog did not get in her way. Keep going. **Your shore is closer than you think!**

Today's Closer Walk

Scripture(s)

For I know the plans I have for you," declares the LORD, "plans to prosper you and not to harm you, plans to give you hope and a future. Jeremiah 29:11

Down the Path

Sure Footing

Your shore is closer than you think. Do not focus on where you are at the moment. Rather, focus on what God plans for you in the future. He is with you. He cares for you and will help you reach your goals.

Solid Ground

Never give up, never give in. Walk with Jesus and where He leads is victory. You will make it. You will succeed, because you are a child of God.

Talking with Jesus

Prayer

Jesus, help me to see that where I am now is not where I am going to stay. Help me keep my eye focused on You and not on my present circumstances. I trust You! Amen.

What are your thoughts as you choose a closer walk with Jesus?

BRUISED, NOT BROKEN

Her story, all too familiar, is a story of loneliness and rejection. Day after day she went about the tasks of her life alone, no friend to talk to, and no ear to listen. Hope was dim. Her life was filled with regret. She was in a hopeless condition. This day started like many other days. She would make her lonely trek to the well to get water for the day. With her head down and her spirit even lower, she began to fill her vessel. Little did she know, her life was about to change forever. Today she was not alone. A stranger asked, "Would you give me a drink of water?" It was Jesus, there at the well to meet her. Jesus saw a need. This woman was in need of fresh water; not the kind of water that quenches one's thirst for a season, but rather, *living water*. He said, "Whoever takes a drink of the water that I will give him shall never, no never, be thirsty any more. But the water that I will give him shall become a spring of water welling up (flowing, bubbling) [continually] within him (into, for) eternal life." (AMP, John, 4:10) "The woman said to Him, Sir, give me this water, so that I may never get thirsty nor have to come [continually all the way] here to draw." (AMP, John 4:15).

Jesus came to heal us, not to break us. Jesus is the gentle shepherd. He knows our pain and our weaknesses. Jesus knew what it was like to be alone and He knew her hurt. She came alone that day to get fresh water. Jesus met her at the well, not to break her but to heal her. He did not say, "Go, and get cleaned up." He did not say, "I don't agree with your lifestyle." He gave her living water, so much that she could not contain it. The dim flicker of her hopeless life became a bright light. The woman left her water jar beside the well and ran back to the village, telling everyone about Jesus, the giver of living water. She did not have to drink the water of hopelessness and rejection, for she had tasted the living water.

When Jesus gives us what we need, we too will leave our water jar of emptiness and hopelessness at the well of ruin and doubt. We will run with joy and victory; we will not be able to contain it. Living water is ours for the taking. Ask for it! Jesus wants to fill us daily. He wants us to run for joy and peace. He is our living water! Let Him fill you today and you too will take off running toward a life filled with joy!

Today's Closer Walk

He heals the broken hearted and binds up their wounds. Psalm 147:3

A bruised reed He will not break, and smoking flax He will not quench, Till He sends forth justice to victory; And in His name Gentiles will trust (Matthew 12:15-21).

Down the Path

Sure Footing

Jesus did not come to break us, He came to fix our broken lives and give us living water so that we will never thirst for the things of this world. Jesus will meet our every need. Trust Him.

Solid Ground

Give your brokenness to Jesus today. He understands your hurt and the challenges you face in life. Jesus wants to heal you and give you joy.

Talking with Jesus

Prayer

Dear Jesus, I want the living water You offer. Jesus, give me living water so that I may never thirst again! Amen.

What are your thoughts as you choose a closer walk with Jesus?

DAY 05

AWESOME GRACE

In a conversation with a friend, I made the comment that God may one day call him into some type of ministry. My friend made a comment that startled me. He said, "God will never use me because I have sinned too much and I'm too weak." I find that many people have this same attitude about God using them in some way or enjoying closer fellowship with Him. Sometimes, I find myself pulled into this thinking. It is possible that the sins of our past and our imperfections are some of the most effective tools the enemy uses against us. He wants to keep us out of fellowship with our Heavenly Father. It's easy to believe that we are not good enough for God. That is why these weapons in the enemy's arsenal are so powerful. The truth is that while we were in sin and separated from God, Christ died for us. Romans 5:8 tells us: "But God put his love on the line for us by offering His Son in sacrificial death while we were of no use whatever to Him. Even when we were separated from God by sin, God sent Jesus to die for us" (NIV). We did not earn what God has so freely given to us through Jesus. God made a way for us to be in fellowship with Him, even while we were useless to him. This awesome act of love is called *Grace*. Through Grace, God illustrates just how much He loves us and cares for us. "Yes!" I told my friend, "You are helpless against your sin and your weaknesses, but through Jesus you are free. Free to fellowship with God and free from the bonds of sin that make you live beneath what God desires for you and what He has given to you through Jesus." Part of God's Grace is His forgiving and forgetting our sin. There is no waiting period for the forgiveness of sins. Once we ask God for forgiveness, it's ours. 1 John 1:9 proclaims: "God is faithful and reliable. If we confess our sins, He forgives them and cleanses us from everything we've done wrong" (NIV). Once we ask for forgiveness, God does not hold our sins against us.

Psalm 130:3 lets us know: "If You, GOD, kept records on wrongdoings, who would stand a chance? As it turns out, forgiveness is your habit" (NIV). We are free through Jesus to be in fellowship with God and to be used by God. Don't live short of what God has so freely given through Jesus. God's grace...receive it.... walk in it...enjoy it! It's yours!

Today's Closer Walk

If you, O LORD, kept a record of sins, O Lord, who could stand? Psalm 130:3

Down the Path

Sure Footing

Our sins, weaknesses and shortcomings have been paid for in full by Jesus. We do not have to live as prisoners to our past sins or as prisoners to our weaknesses and shortcomings.

Solid Ground

Only Jesus can change us through the power of the Holy Spirit. Lay your sins at the foot of the cross and pick up the grace and forgiveness Jesus gives us so freely. Don't let your weaknesses stand in the way of your fellowship with Jesus.

Talking with Jesus

Prayer

Dear Lord, thank You that my sins are forgiven through Jesus. Help me to walk in Your grace today. Amen.

What are your thoughts as you choose a closer walk with Jesus?

DAY 06

CHOOSE LIFE

Yogi Berra, the famous New York Yankees baseball player, once said, "When you come to a fork in the road, take it." When it comes to making decisions, this quote sums up how difficult it is to make a level-headed decision. In Deuteronomy 30:19, God places two choices before us: "Look at what I've done for you today: I've placed in front of you Life and Good, Death and Evil." God says, "Look, here it is, life or death; you choose". Many of our decisions in life boil down to these two choices. Each time we make a decision or choose which direction our lives will go, we must consider: am I choosing life and good or death and evil? If we choose life, what does that mean for us? Dueteronomy 30:9 tells us that God will outdo himself in making things go well for us. God wants what is good for us; he wants to bless us beyond our comprehension. He wants us to realize our hopes and dreams. "No eye has seen, no ear has heard, and no mind has imagined the things that God has prepared for those who love him" (NIV, I Cor. 2:9). This is what it means to choose life. God will outdo himself in bringing blessings to our lives. It does not mean that every decision we make is a life or death decision. If we make choices contrary to God's word and will, we will begin to see the things of God wear away and fade. In the long run, death and evil will be the result. So choose the path for your life that will bring life and glorify God. When we are faced with a decision to forgive or not to forgive, we need to consider this: if we do not forgive, does this line up with the word of God? Will this decision bring life to my life? Will God outdo himself to bless me if I do not forgive? When God says "give," and we choose to give, will giving bring life and good? In Luke 6:38, Jesus says "Give, and it shall be given unto you; good measure, pressed down, and shaken together, and running over, shall men give into your bosom" (NIV). The decision to give brings life and good and God will outdo himself to bless us. In Deuteronomy 30:19, God says, "I have put in front of you life and death, the good and the curse. So choose life so you and your children after you may live" (NIV). God, who created heaven and earth, commands us to choose life. What is your choice?

Today's Closer Walk

But if serving the LORD seems undesirable to you, then choose for yourselves this day whom you will serve, whether the gods your forefathers served beyond the River, or the gods of the Amorites, in whose land you are living. But as for me and my household, we will serve the LORD." Joshua 24:15

Down the Path

Sure Footing

God's word tells us that He will out do Himself in making things well for us if we choose life. Today, make decisions based on the life-giving word of God. Choose life.

Solid Ground

Decide today that you will choose to walk according to God's word and principals and you will be blessed because of it. You will walk in fellowship with Jesus when you choose life.

Talking with Jesus

Prayer

Lord Jesus, I choose life today! When I need to forgive, I'll forgive. When I need to love, I'll love. I follow Your example of choosing life. Amen.

What are your thoughts as you choose a closer walk with Jesus?

DAY 07

DETAILS, DETAILS, DETAILS

My wife and I are considering building our next home. To say there are a lot of details in this process is an understatement. First, there is the lot or land to consider. How much will it cost? What's the right location? Then, the house plan; what kind of house should we build? Should it be a single level, split-level, or ranch style? Next, there is the contractor. In our area there are only a *couple hundred thousand* to choose from! In addition to the major decisions, there are all the minor decisions for example: paint colors, carpet colors, or are we going with hard wood floors? Kitchen cabinets, do we want natural wood or painted cabinets? The details of this project are endless and tiring to think about. It would be foolish to start a project like building a house without working out most of the details in advance. God's building plan for our lives is much different. God wants us to trust Him with the details of our lives, all the details. Most of us want a detailed plan from God in advance. We say, "Yes Lord, I'll follow you as long as you give me an in-depth plan and let me know in advance what to expect and where I will be going and what I will find and do when I get there." God expects and commands that we walk in faith. Hebrews 11:6 explains: "But where there is no faith it is impossible to please Him; for the man who draws near to God must believe that there is a God and that He proves Himself a rewarder of those who earnestly try to find Him" (NIV). By faith, we follow God. We will not know the full plan that God has for our lives, but we know the one who gives the plan. The key to walking in faith is to draw near to God daily in prayer, praise, and in the study of his word. "Faith comes by hearing and hearing by the word of God" (NIV, Romans 10:17) The more we know God and His nature, the more we know He cares for us and will not let us down. "Casting the whole of your care all your anxieties, all your worries, all your concerns, once and for all on Him, for He cares for you affectionately and cares about you watchfully" (AMP, I Peter 5:7). God will always do what is best for us as his children. Our part in our relationship with God is to trust Him completely, live in faith, and leave the details of the plan for our lives to our Heavenly Father.

Proverbs 3:5-6 gives us great advice in following God: "First, Trust in the lord with all thine heart. Second, lean not to your own understanding. Don't try to figure out what God is up to; just trust Him. Third, in all your ways acknowledge him and he will direct thy paths one step at a time" (NIV). Jeremiah 29:11 sums up what God has promised for us: "I know what I'm doing. I have it all planned out—plans to take care of you, not abandon you, plans to give you the future you hope for" (NIV). We will not always know God's plan for our lives but we know

God, and in this we can rest. In him we can trust that He will take care of us. We know God who has the plan. Trust Him.

Today's Closer Walk

Cast all your anxiety on him because he cares for you. I Peter 5:7

Down the Path

Sure Footing

No matter what our circumstances are or how we may feel, God has the full plan for our life and future. He is teaching us to trust Him completely.

Solid Ground

My Grandmother often said, "Let go and let God." Let go of what you think God should do and trust that He is working on your behalf to make every area of your life glorify Him.

Talking with Jesus

Prayer

Dear Lord, I put my trust in You! Teach me to see how You are working in my life. Amen.

What are your thoughts as you choose a closer walk with Jesus?

WHY ARE YOU SO AFRAID
MARK 4:36-40

The storm was brutal. The winds blew with enormous force. The waves poured into their boat. It seemed as if all would be lost. Jesus' disciples woke Him, saying, "Teacher, is it nothing to You that we're going down? Do You not care that we are perishing?" Many times in our walk with Jesus, this describes how we feel and is at times exactly where we find ourselves. We ask: God, where are You? Don't You care about me? Lord, don't You know that the car payment is due and I don't have the money? Lord, don't You care about my children? I have been praying for them and still they are not walking with You. Lord, I have been praying for healing for so long; when will I be healed? It seems at times that whatever could go wrong, does go wrong. Sometimes circumstances overwhelm us. When we focus on the winds of adversity and the waves of fear rather than the mighty wind of the Holy Spirit, our world sinks into anxiety and doubt. Jesus was in the same boat with His disciples. He was in the same storm. But where was He? Asleep! Jesus was at peace. He had so much trust that His life was in His Fathers hands that He could sleep through the storm. Jesus responded to the cry of his disciples. He got up, rebuked the wind, and said to the waves, "Quiet! Be still!" The wind died down, and when all was calm, Jesus asked of his disciples. "Why are you so afraid? Do you still have no faith?" He asks the question as if to say, "You have no reason to be afraid. I am with you. Why are you so anxious and troubled?" Jesus promised never to leave us or forsake us. He said, "Fear thou not, for I am with thee, be not dismayed, for I am thy God; I strengthen thee, yea, I help thee; yea, I uphold thee with My victorious right hand." (Isaiah 41:10) God himself commands us not to fear. He says, "I am your God!" I will uphold thee! Why then do we fear? When the storms of life come here is what we should do. **First, fear not,** know that God is with you and cares about you." 1 Peter 5:7 tells us: "Throw the whole of your anxiety upon Him, because He Himself cares for you. **Second, don't be dismayed,** distraught, troubled or sad. Know that God is in control." Proverbs 3:5 says, "Trust the LORD with all your heart, and do not rely on your own understanding." **Third, seek daily strength** from God. Isaiah 12:2, "Yes, indeed God is my salvation. I trust, I won't be afraid. God yes God! Is my strength and song, best of all, my salvation!" When we purpose in our hearts to totally rely on God as our strength He will speak to our storms. The winds of anxiety and fear will die down and God will make our storm completely calm.

Today's Closer Walk

The LORD is my rock, my fortress and my deliverer; my God is my rock, in whom I take refuge. He is my shield and the horn of my salvation, my stronghold. Psalm 18:2

Down the Path

Sure Footing

We do not have to be overtaken with fear when the storms of life come Jesus is always near. His protection is ours. We are carved on the palm of his hand.

Solid Ground

Psalm 73:28 David said it is good for me to draw near to God. I have put my trust in the Lord God that I may declare all thy works. Draw near to Jesus and when the storms of life try to overtake our faith.

Talking with Jesus

Prayer

Lord, you are my rock and my fortress. I put my trust in you. I thank you that today, you kept me safe.

What are your thoughts as you choose a closer walk with Jesus?

DAY 09

INTO THE STORM

During a hurricane the Air Force Reserve's 53rd Weather Reconnaissance Squadron deploys its aircraft to fly directly into the hurricane to gather data. This data will tell the national weather service how strong the storm is and what direction the storm may follow. The data gathered is valuable to those in the path of the storm and to those around the storm. The information gained from flying directly into the storm makes the dangerous trip valuable for **much is to be gained by this journey**. The trip is worth the risk. The aircraft and flight crew fly directly into the hurricane. In a typical mission they fly into the storm a half dozen times. They don't fly around the storm. They don't fly above the storm. They don't avoid the storm. They head right for the heart of the storm. The flight crew is not surprised when they get a call to fly into a hurricane, as a matter of fact; the crew expects this kind of mission. The flight crew does not ask their commander to reassign them or ask, "Why us?" They don't moan and groan or ask how long this will last. The crew eagerly takes on the task at hand. They know the ride will be rough and challenging. The winds will shift the aircraft will rock back and forth and the crew knows this ride will not be comfortable. They expect a rough ride.

Jesus said, "In this world you will have tribulation." He might have said, "Your mission as my disciples will be tough you will have to head directly into life's storms." Jesus did not sugar coat, gloss over, or try to make us think that our walk with him would be easy. Our walk is filled with peace and Joy, but at times it is difficult. The word tribulation means: great affliction, trial, distress and even suffering. In James 1:2-4, says, "Count it all joy when we encounter trials and testing. Consider it a sheer gift, friends, when tests and challenges come at you from all sides." You know that under pressure, your faith-life is forced into the open and shows its true colors. The testing of our faith develops our faith. Tests and trails deepen our relationship with God. It is through the valley of shadow of death that we realize that we do not have to fear because we know God is with us.

When we face difficult times and situations, when the night is the darkest, and we have to strain to see hope, the peace that passes all understanding comes to us and will keep or guard our hearts and minds in Christ. Just as the information gained from flying directly a hurricane makes the dangerous trip valuable and much will be gained by the journey. We can handle life's storms without fear. We know that step-by-step, moment-by-moment, our God is with us. He promised that he would never leave us or forsake us and he would be with us to the end of the earth. (Matt. 28:20) It is in the journey not the destination where our faith is deepened. It is in this journey that we realize the deep unconditional love our Lord has for us, as well as, his awesome power working in our behalf. When life's storms come we are not alone. If God is for us who can be against us?

Today's Closer Walk

No, despite all these things, overwhelming victory is ours through Christ, who loved us. Romans 8:37

Down the Path

Sure Footing

Tests, trials, difficult situations will come our way, there is no way to avoid them, many times trying to avoid storms brings more anxiety than facing them head on. Remember we are more than conquers through Christ Jesus and Jesus will lead the way to victory.

Solid Ground

Instead of looking at challenges that come our way with dread, look at what we will learn through the process of overcoming life's tribulations. There is much to learn and in the end toe journey will be worth the struggle.

Talking with Jesus

Prayer

Dear Jesus, I stand on your word that says you will be with me always even when in the natural I can't feel your presence, I know you're there. Help me to see what you would have me to learn through every challenge.

What are your thoughts as you choose a closer walk with Jesus?

DAY 10

FOR IN HIM WE LIVE AND MOVE
AND HAVE OUR BEING

Jesus said "I tell you the truth, the Son can do nothing by himself; he can do only what he sees his father doing, because whatever the Father does the son also does". (John 5: 19) As followers of Jesus, we must daily seek to live like Jesus lived. Jesus lived in the Father's presence; He was in constant fellowship with his Father. Jesus knew the Father and **Jesus always had what He needed when He needed it**. Jesus had a healing touch of sight for a blind man and forgiveness for a woman caught in her sin. Jesus gave hope and peace to a world dying in its sin. Jesus touched the world through his relationship with the Father. The way we will touch the world around us is through our fellowship with our Heavenly Father. Jesus freely gave his life for the world because it was the will of his Father. As followers of Christ we must seek to know our Lord, so much so, that we do what we see our Lord doing. We love like our Lord loves; we touch the world like our Lord wants the world to be touched. Jesus lived and moved and had his being in the Father. He said, "I and my Father are one." (John 10:30) The world needs salvation and the hope, peace, and love that salvation brings. His Spirit will touch the world through us. Those who know Jesus, those who move and have their being in Him, will touch the world in a mighty way. For in Him, we live and move and have our being.

Today's Closer Walk

Verily, verily, I say unto you, He that believeth on me, the works that I do shall he do also; and greater works than these shall he do; because I go unto my Father. John 14:12

Down the Path

Sure Footing

It is through fellowship with Jesus that we too will have what we need when we need it. As we live and move in our daily lives let us seek to do what Jesus did. Jesus could only do what he did because of his close fellowship with the Father.

Solid Ground

Give your daily life to Jesus. Give the grind that we sometimes find ourselves in to him, even in the seemingly routine tasks of our lives Jesus wants to touch, love, and heal through us.

Talking with Jesus

Prayer

Dear Lord Jesus, show me the people that you want to touch through me today. What are your thoughts as you choose a closer walk with Jesus?

DAY 11

WHY DAVID RAN

In the account of David and Goliath, one of the most popular stories of the Old Testament, we see the army of Israel in a standoff with the Philistine army. The Philistine's fierce warrior Goliath taunted the army of Israel for 40 days. Goliath, the giant, was 9 feet tall. Goliath said, "I defy the ranks of Israel this day; give me a man, that we may fight together." When Saul and all Israel heard the words of the Philistine, they were dismayed and greatly afraid. No man out of all the mighty men in the army of Israel had the courage to face this mighty giant. In contrast, we see David, a young man sent to take his brothers food on the battlefield. David was a shepherd tending his father's sheep, a boy. David arrives on the battlefield and upon hearing about Goliath taunting and challenging the army of Israel, David said, "who is this uncircumcised Philistine that he should defy the armies of the living God?" David convinces Saul to allow him to fight the giant. David tells Saul, "I have killed both the lion and the bear; and this uncircumcised Philistine shall be like one of them, for he has defied the armies of the living God!" Saul agrees to allow David to fight Goliath. When Goliath came forward to meet him, an amazing thing happened, David **ran** quickly toward the battle line to meet the Philistine.

Here is where I want to pose a question, **why** was David able to run to meet the enemy? Why was there no fear in David? **Why** was there no doubt? **Why** was victory so sure in David's mind? **What** would motivate someone to run into a battle that even his own family said he could not win? The answer is the same for you and me. We can **run** to face our enemy just like David. The same reason we do not have to live in fear. The same reason we can have assurance and not doubt. The same reason we can be sure of victory. The same reason we can stand tall in the face of any adversity or challenge. The same reason we can walk through the valley of the shadow of death and fear no evil. David lived and moved and had his being in God.

David made his dwelling in the secret place of the Most High. God was his fortress, his rock and strong hold. David knew God, That's the answer! Today, we have the answer. His name is Jesus.

What are you waiting for? Run! Run to face your enemy! The enemy of need and doubt, the enemy of depression, the enemy of lust, the enemy that steals your faith, the enemy of your finances, Run! You can! God will give you your victory through Jesus, The Author and finisher of our faith. Victory is today!

Today's Closer Walk

But thanks be to God, which giveth us the victory through our Lord Jesus Christ.
I Corinthians 15:57

Down the Path

Sure Footing

David knew and walked with God. David ran to meet Goliath because he knew
he would win. David faced Goliath in the name of the Lord God Almighty.
We must face our giants the same way. Victory is ours through the Lord God
Almighty. He is our Lord!

Solid Ground

Let the fear of loosing go, Jesus does not loose. We will overcome we will have
victory. Let go of fear and let God lead you to victory!

Talking with Jesus

Prayer

Jesus, help me to take courage in the fact that I don't have to fear what giants lie
ahead. I know and trust your delivering power.

What are your thoughts as you choose a closer walk with Jesus?

DAY 12

LIFE COMES AT YOU FAST

A slogan of a popular insurance company is, "Life comes at you fast" The message of this slogan is: you never know what you are going to face in the next moment. Life is just that way at times. One minute things are moving along just fine and in the next minute, life comes at you hard. Our faith is tested by an unexpected trial. The car breaks down at the wrong time. The dog eats your homework, for real this time. A deadline is approaching and it looks like there is no way to make it. A sudden illness strikes and we wonder what to do. We need more than just a good insurance policy; we need divine **assurance.** We may not know what we will face in the next moment of life, but we know who holds the next moment. David puts it best in Psalm 139: "Lord, you ... know all about me you know when I sit down and when I get up. You know my thoughts before I think them. You know where I go and where I lie down. You know thoroughly everything I do. Lord, even before I say a word, you already know it. You are all around me in front and in back and have put **your hand** on me. Your knowledge is amazing to me; it is more than I can understand." Even when life comes at us hard it does not surprise God. David says, "God is in front and in back of me. He knows what is ahead of us and he is already there to protect
us. God is in control of every moment of our lives." Jesus said, "The very hairs of your head are all numbered." (Matt. 10:30) If God knows how many hairs there on your head, you can rest assured he cares about every part of your life. Another insurance company declares, "You are in good hands." As Christians we are in good hands and have divine **assurance.** We are in God's hands, the best hands of all. In Isaiah 49: 15-16 God says, "I will not forget you. Behold, I have engraved you on the palms of my hands" How awesome to know that, when life comes at us hard and the world seems to be bringing challenges on all sides, we are carved on the hands of God. Our divine **assurance** is that God will never leave us nor forsake us. Psalm 125:1 proclaims: "Those who trust in GOD are like Zion Mountain: Nothing can move it, a rock-solid mountain you can always depend on."

Mountains encircle Jerusalem , GOD encircles his people. He always has and always will. We are engraved on the palm of God's hand. We have divine assurance. We are not alone. God orders our steps. God leads us to victory. Psalm 91 declares: "The Almighty will protect those who go to God Most High for safety, when life comes at us hard. God is our place of safety and protection. God will save us from hidden traps and from deadly diseases. He will cover us with his feathers, and under his wings we can hide. His truth will be our shield and protection." When life comes at us hard we have **assurance.** We are in good hands. "I have engraved you on the palms of my hands," says God, "I will never forget you." Go, live your life in victory!

Today's Closer Walk

For I, saith the LORD, will be unto her a wall of fire round about, and will be the glory in the midst of her. Zechariah 2:5

Down the Path

Sure Footing

Remember; nothing that you will go through is going to take God by surprise. God knows what is ahead and is there to provide protection as well as what you need to make it through any situation.

Solid Ground

Thank God that he sees what we cannot. When it seems like we are facing life's challenges that seem to appear out of nowhere, trust him.

Talking with Jesus

Prayer

Lord, your are my rock and my fortress and I trust in you to keep me safe in all of life's challenges.

What are your thoughts as you choose a closer walk with Jesus?

DAY 13

LET IT SHINE

I once took a tour of Mammoth Cave in Kentucky. At one point during the tour, our tour guide turned off the lights; there was complete and total darkness. It was so dark I could not see my hand in front of my face. Everything disappeared. The tour guide lit a match; from this small flame the massive cave was illuminated. I was awestruck at the power that the small flickering light created. One small flame overpowered the darkest darkness I had ever experienced. I realized that no matter how dark, or how dense the darkness, it could not overpower the tiniest flame. There simply was no amount of darkness that could ever overpower this light. Jesus said in John 9:5, "I am the Light of the world." As Christians, we are in Jesus; we are His living body in this world. Therefore, we are also lights. Jesus said in Matthew 5:14, "You are the light of the world". No matter what darkness we face and no matter how dark the darkness may get, it will never overtake the light of Jesus that is in us. Jesus said in Matthew 5:16, "Let your light shine before men, that they may see your good works, and may glorify your Father who is in the heavens." Jesus said, "Let your light shine." Be who you are in Jesus. We are his body. We are his hands that touch and bring healing to the dark world around us. We are his mouthpieces to speak love and forgiveness to those who are trapped in the dark cave of loneliness and frustration. We are his feet to go into all parts of the world, as He commands, to preach the Good News of salvation. Here's another way to put it: "You're here to be light, bringing out the God colors in the world... be generous with your lives. By opening up to others, you'll prompt people to open up with God, this generous Father in heaven." (Matthew 5:16 MSG) Let your light shine. It only takes a small flickering flame to illuminate the lives of those around us. Let your light shine!

Today's Closer Walk

In him was life; and the life was the light of men. John 1:4

Down the Path

Sure Footing

Jesus is the light of the world. We have his light in us and darkness can not over power his light in us. When the light of Jesus shines through us the whole world see's and darkness must flee!

Solid Ground

Jesus said, "Let you light shine." Today, be who you are in Jesus and let his light shine through you. Don't make it shine, LET IT SHINE!

Talking with Jesus

Prayer

Dear Jesus, let you light shine through me so that the world around me can see your marvelous light.

What are your thoughts as you choose a closer walk with Jesus?

LOVE ME MORE

In Mark chapter 10, a rich young man ran to Jesus and fell on his knees before Jesus. The man asked, "Good teacher what must I do to have life forever?" Jesus answered, "Why do you call me good? Only God is good. You know the commandments: You must not murder anyone. You must not be guilty of adultery. You must not steal. You must not tell lies about your neighbor. You must not cheat. Honor your father and mother." This young man was looking for a way to eternal life. He was looking to Jesus for the answer. He was in the right place to get his question answered. The young man answered, "'Teacher, I have obeyed all these things since I was a boy.' Jesus, looking at the man, loved him and said, 'There is one more thing you need to do. Go and sell everything you have, and give it to the poor: you will have treasure in heaven. Then come and follow me.' The young man was very sad to hear Jesus say this, and he left very sorrowfully, because he was rich."

There is a difference in what we want and what we are willing to do for the things we desire. The young man desired eternal life. He did what he thought he needed to do to attain it but it was not enough. His riches stood between him and Jesus. We as followers of Christ must abandon all that stands between Jesus and us. We need to sell out and follow him. Jesus is saying to the rich young man, and us, "Love me more than your riches." The greatest command is to love the Lord our God with everything we have.

Today's Closer Walk

But seek ye first the kingdom of God, and his righteousness; and all these things shall be added unto you. Matthew 6:33

Down the Path

Sure Footing

Doing for God does not equal fellowship with God. Following rules does not always lead to a greater understanding of God. Works and rules do have their place in life but can get in the way of truly knowing God.

Solid Ground

Let us examine our lives today and let Jesus move all the things that stand in the way of greater fellowship with him. Jesus wants our love first.

Talking with Jesus

Prayer

Dear Jesus, I freely give up all the things that stand in the way of greater fellowship with you. Help me to recognize the things that I must part with.

What are your thoughts as you choose a closer walk with Jesus?

DAY 15

WHAT DO YOU SEE

The human eye, wonderfully created by God, can only focus on one thing at a time. Stand on a high ridge and look out over a mountain range with all of the different colors, the snow capped mountains. One sees an overabundance of unique scenery. However the eye can only focus on one aspect of this beautiful scenery .God created our eye by design so that we could only focus on one thing at a time. God wants us to see many things but he only wants us to focus on one thing at a time, not just anything, **the right thing**. In Matthew 6:22 Jesus said, "The light of the body is the eye: if therefore thine eye be single, thy whole body shall be full of light". When the trials of life come our way what will we focus on? When we are challenged with difficult circumstances will our eye be single? Will we focus on the "author and finisher of our faith" to see how God will bring light into our circumstance? When our faith is tested will we overcome by focusing on the strength and courage God has provided in his Word and through his Holy Spirit? "Look at the wildflowers. They never primp or shop, but have you ever seen color and design quite like it? The ten best-dressed men and women in the country look shabby alongside them. If God gives such attention to the appearance of wildflowers—most of which are never even seen—don't you think he'll attend to you, take pride in you, do his best for you? What I'm trying to do here is to get you to relax, to not be so preoccupied with *getting*, so you can respond to God's *giving*. People who don't know God and the way he works fuss over these things, but you know both God and how he works. Steep your life in God-reality, God-initiative, God-provisions. Don't worry about missing out. You'll find all your everyday human concerns will be met." (Matt 6:20-33 the Message) Do not focus on the problems and worries of this life. Focus on the promises and blessings that God has so richly bestowed upon us. When we focus on all the good things God has given us, how could we possibly worry?

Today's Closer Walk

See to it, then, that the light within you is not darkness. Luke 11:35

Down the Path

Sure Footing

Do you see the glass half full or half empty? God always see's you as a full vessel ready to show forth his glory! Focus on what God says about you! You are a chosen vessel for God. Let him glorify himself in you!

Solid Ground

Do not focus on the challenges and worries of this life. Focus on the strength and courage you have within you as a child of God. His provision for you is always present.

Talking with Jesus

Prayer

Lord Jesus, I only have eyes for you! Help me to see what you have provided for me and not on what I don't have.

What are your thoughts as you choose a closer walk with Jesus?

DAY 16

MORE OF THE STORY

We have all heard the legendary Paul Harvey end his moving stories about inspiring people with the words, "and now you know the rest of the story". The apostle Paul is an example of just the kind of person Paul Harvey would talk about. The apostle Paul was an inspiring person. Paul's impact in the history of Christianity is incredibly important. He was one of the first preachers to preach the Good News of Jesus Christ to the Gentile world (that's us folks) he is also the author of more New Testament books than any other biblical writer. The Apostle Paul spent roughly one quarter of his missionary career in prisons. It is in prison that many of his letters were written. The conditions in prison were less than desirable, to say the least. Roman imprisonment, for example, was preceded by being stripped naked and then flogged, a humiliating, painful, and bloody ordeal (Acts 16:22-24). The bleeding wounds went untreated as prisoners sat in painful leg or wrist chains. Shredded bloodstained clothing was not replaced, even in the cold of winter. Most cells were dark, especially the inner cells of a prison, like the one Paul and Silas occupied in Philippi. (Acts 16) Agonizing cold, lack of water, cramped quarters, and the sickening stench from few toilets made sleeping difficult and waking hours miserable. Because of the miserable conditions, many prisoners begged for a speedy death. Others simply committed suicide. In settings like this, Paul wrote encouraging, even joyful, letters. From prison Paul wrote, "Always be joyful in the Lord! I'll say it again: Be joyful!" (Philippians 4:4) The message translation puts it this way: "Celebrate God all day, every day. I mean, revel in him! Make it as clear as you can to all you meet..." Denied of freedom and most of life's comforts, Paul, so grateful and joyful in his relationship with Jesus wrote, "Celebrate God." It is clear that Paul, our inspiration, celebrated God. It is from prison that Paul tells us this. Why? Because it is the way he lived motivated by his love for Jesus. Do we love Jesus so much so that we would celebrate him even in the worst circumstances?

Paul knew Jesus. He considered it a sheer joy to be counted as a follower and bondservant of Jesus. (Romans 1:1) Paul rejoiced in the Lord in all situations, even in the dark, cold, inner cell of a Roman prison. Paul also said in 1 Corinthians 11:1, "Be imitators of me, in so far as I in turn am an imitator of Christ." As we go through our life in Christ we need to celebrate God in every situation. Seek him first in all that we do and love him with all of our hearts. We need to make it clear to the world around us that no matter what comes our way or what challenges we face, nothing will stop us from celebrating Jesus. When we do this, we will affect the world around us. **Those God places in our world will want to meet the Jesus we know and celebrate.** Now you know... more of the story!

Today's Closer Walk

And they worshipped him, and returned to Jerusalem with great joy: Luke 24:52

Down the Path

Sure Footing

Paul the great man that he was gave us great advice, "Always be joyful in the Lord!" Our joy should not be hindered by the circumstances we find ourselves in. The world will see that the joy we have is real joy. Our real joy will lead others to Christ.

Solid Ground

Make it clear to the world around us and each other that no matter what comes our way or what challenges we face nothing will stop us from celebrating Jesus!

Talking with Jesus

Prayer

Jesus, I rejoice in you! You are my Joy! Let the world see your joy in me!

What are your thoughts as you choose a closer walk with Jesus?

DAY 17

OODLES OF POWER AND COMFORT

Tim, A good friend of mine, began to enlighten me about the new truck he had just bought. He told me about the features of his truck; the towing capacity, the torque, engine size, how many pounds the truck would haul and how comfortable the ride is. Tim was a proud owner of a truck with *oodles* of power and comfort (I'm not sure how much is *oodles*, but it must be a lot!). When he finished, I wondered, what one could do with all that power and comfort? For another hour I listened to Tim expound on the scores of uses for all the features of his truck. I began to think about the power and comfort we have as Christians. What could we do with the power and comfort Jesus gave us as his followers? Jesus said, "You will receive power when the Holy Spirit has come upon you, and you shall be My witnesses in Jerusalem and all Judea and Samaria and to the ends of the earth." (Acts 1:8) With the power Jesus gave us, we are empowered to be his witnesses to this world. The world will see that we live above and not beneath in every situation. With the power Jesus gave us we can be in the right place at the right time all the time. The world will see that we have victory over the cares of the world. Our lives are filled with joy and peace. Our day-to-day lives will be a living testimony to the world in which we live and the world around us will desire to know the God we serve. The power Jesus spoke of literally means ability, efficiency and might. It is the ability to rise above any situation we face in order to glorify God. It is the efficiency to convey the gospel message in the best way to the many diverse people. The might or strength in our inner being is for us to know how to pray and not grow weak or faint when we are faced with the world's challenges. Jesus said we must always pray, and not give up. (Luke 18:1) Jesus also said we would not be left comfortless he said, "I will pray to the Father, and he shall give you another Comforter, that he may abide with you for ever." If there is one thing that the world needs it is comfort. If there is one thing we need when we face tough situations it is comfort.

We are promised that the Comforter will never leave us; he will be with us forever. One does not have to look very far to see the hurt and pain that is all around. As people that have received power from the Holy Sprit, we are to bring the hope of comfort to a hurting, lonely, dying world. Through the power of the Holy Spirit, God works through us and in us to accomplish his plan and purpose for our lives and this world. Tim was a proud owner of a truck with *oodles* of power and comfort. We are a people with *oodles* of power and comfort from the Holy Sprit. Let's go out into the world and let God work through us!

Today's Closer Walk

Scripture(s)

Shout for joy, O heavens; rejoice, O earth; burst into song, O mountains! For the LORD comforts his people and will have compassion on his afflicted ones. Isaiah 49:13

Down the Path

Sure Footing

Jesus left us with a comforter and oodles of peace! With the power of Jesus we can be in the right place at the right time all of the time and touch the world around us.

Solid Ground

Rest in what God gave us. His power, His peace, His comfort, His victory. All he has is ours, for we are his children.

Talking with Jesus

Prayer

Lord Jesus I thank you for what you have given me to be able to live above and not beneath! Fill me today with your spirit so that I may glorify YOU!

What are your thoughts as you choose a closer walk wit

DAY 18

PEACE, TAKE IT! LIVE IN IT! IT'S YOURS!

In our world everyone seems to be in a chase for peace. We say if I have enough money, I'll have peace. If I meet the right person, I'll have peace. If I had a better job, I would have peace. If my children would stay on the right path, I would have peace. If I could just have one more spiritual experience, I would have peace. The list could go on and on. We reach for what we think will bring us peace and just when we think we have it, it slips further and further away. It reminds me of the song, "looking for love in all the wrong places." But instead of love, it is peace we are looking for "in all the wrong places." We cannot have peace if we look for it in the world. Our peace comes from the Rock of our salvation, Jesus. Jesus said: "Peace I leave with you; **My [own] peace** I now give and bequeath to you. **Not as the world gives** do I give to you." (John 14:27). What better peace to have than the peace of Jesus. Not just any kind of peace but HIS PEACE, he said, "I'm giving you my peace, you don't have to work for it or earn it I'm giving it to you! Take it! Live in It! It's yours!"

Some of the keys to living and abiding in peace are: Give your entire attention to what God is doing right now, and don't get worked up about what may or may not happen tomorrow. God will help you deal with whatever hard things come up when the time comes Matthew 6:33. Don't worry. It is easier said than done. Try this. Instead of worrying, pray. Let petitions and praises shape your worries into prayers, letting God know your concerns. Before you know it, a sense of God's wholeness, everything coming together for good, will come and settle you down. It's wonderful what happens when Christ displaces worry at the center of your life. (Philippians 4:7) When we pray and cast our cares on Jesus, He keeps us in perfect peace, not just adequate peace or peace that let's us sleep, but perfect peace!

With perfect peace you will protect those whose minds cannot be changed, because they trust you, (Isaiah26: 3). Keep your focus on Jesus, not on your problems, not on the negative, not on the storms of life; keep your focus on the author and finisher of your faith. Summing it all up, friends, I'd say you'll do best by filling your minds and meditating on things true, noble, reputable, authentic, compelling, gracious—the best, not the worst; the beautiful, not the ugly; things to praise, not things to curse, (Philippians 4:8).

HIS PEACE, Jesus said I'm giving you my peace; you don't have to work for it or earn it I'm giving it to you! Take it! Live in It! It's yours! What are you waiting for? Peace is today!

Today's Closer Walk

Scripture(s)

Whatever you have learned or received or heard from me, or seen in me—put it into practice. And the God of peace will be with you. Philippians 4:9

Down the Path

Sure Footing

We can not have peace if we look for it in the world. We must rely on the pease that Jesus already gave us! We don't have to work for it like the world wants us to believe, all we have to do is accept it!

Solid Ground

Don't chase peace, let the peace of Jesus overtake you! Jesus said, "Here, it's yours!" Live in it by faith, accept his peace as your own because it is!

Talking with Jesus

Prayer

Lord Jesus , I accept your peace as my own. I thank you that you have given it to me. I love you!

What are your thoughts as you choose a closer walk with Jesus?

DAY 19

SAME OLE SAME OLE

When asked, "How are you doing?" or "How's it going?" some people will say, "Same ole same ole" or "Same thing, just a different day". Sometimes it seems as if life is just grinding along with not many changes or excitement. We get up in the morning and drink our coffee. We eat our breakfast and go through our daily routine just like we did yesterday. It is hard to see God at work at times. It's easy to let discouragement creep in and make us think our life is just a grind, a dull routine, or a holding pattern. When we find our life in this pattern we need to remember that God created us for a purpose and that He has a plan for our lives. Each day there are lives for us to touch. Each day has purpose. Someone, during our daily routines, needs our touch. Remember, today is not yesterday. Yesterday is gone and it will never be again. Today is living and breathing. Today is bright and new. Today is full of God's purpose and plan for our lives. Take your everyday, ordinary life—your sleeping, eating, going-to-work, and walking-around life—and place it before God as an offering. Embracing what God does for you is the best thing you can do for Him. Fix your attention on God. You will be changed from the inside out. Recognize what He wants from you, and quickly respond to it. (Romans 12)

When we are tempted to think life is a grind and discouragement tries to rear its ugly head, there are a few things we need to realize. First, God's love never ceases towards us; He is working in us and through us to bring into reality his plan for our lives and that his mercies are new every day. (Lam. 3:22-23) In addition, the Lord orders our steps. Psalm 37:23 says," The LORD directs the steps of the godly. He delights in every detail of their lives." God is in the details; He cares about our day-to-day routines and delights in them. Next, the very steps we take come from GOD, otherwise how would we know where we're going? (Proverbs 20:24) It's hard to think of our lives as a grind when the steps we take come from God. If Jesus were to meet you in the midst of your daily routine and ask, "How's it going?" How are you going to respond?

Today's Closer Walk

Scripture(s)

God's loyal love couldn't have run out, his merciful love couldn't have dried up. They're created new every morning. How great your faithfulness! Lamentations 3:22-23

Down the Path

Sure Footing

As children of God we have a purpose, , even on a Monday when life seems to grind along. God has someone for you to touch, love, or even bring healing to. The world may say that we just grind along until we stop, but God says everyday has a divine purpose!

Solid Ground

Embrace Monday, embrace what you think is, "The Grind" fellowship with Jesus and allow him to work in you the plan he has for you life today. Your life is never a grind. God does direct your steps!

Talking with Jesus

Prayer

Thank you Father that you direct my steps! And that today will not be a grind but will be wonderful because you and I fellowship together!

What are your thoughts as you choose a closer walk with Jesus?

DAY 20

THE DISEASE OF BEING UNWANTED

Mother Teresa, whose sisters in Calcutta run both a hospice and a clinic for leprosy patients, once said, "We have drugs for people with diseases like leprosy. But these drugs do not treat the main problem, the disease of being unwanted. That's what my sisters hope to provide." The sick and the poor, she said, suffer even more from rejection than material want. Jesus said in Luke 4:18, "The Spirit of the Lord is with me. He has anointed me to tell the Good News to the poor. He has sent me to announce forgiveness to the prisoners of sin and the restoring of sight to the blind, to forgive those who have been shattered by sin." Jesus came to touch those who suffered from the disease of being unwanted. Jesus reached out to touch and give life to a leper and those whose lives have been marked by rejection. A leper was perhaps the most unwanted and down cast of all. In the times in which Jesus lived, very few people would have anything to do with a leper. Levitical laws decreed that a person with leprosy live outside the town, keep a six- foot distance from everyone else, and wear the clothes of a mourner. Jesus came to reach all that were hurting, even the leper. When a man with leprosy came to Jesus, Jesus reached out his hand and touched the man. This touch from Jesus gave new life to man whose life was marked by rejection. Jesus came to reach the poor, and those who were prisoners of sin; he came to piece together, and even restore, shattered lives. In the seventh chapter of Luke, the disciples of John the Baptist asked Jesus, "Are You the One Who is to come, or shall we continue to look for another? Jesus said, "Go back and give news to John of what you have seen, and the things which have come to your ears; the blind now see, those who had no power in their legs are walking, lepers are made clean, those who had no hearing now have their ears open, dead men come to life again, and the poor have the good news given to them." Jesus said, "Look at what I am doing; I am doing what I was sent here to do. I have come to give abundant life." As followers of Jesus we are His hands, His feet, His touch, His body.

Those whose lives are suffering from the disease of being unwanted are the lives we are to touch. Just as Jesus did, we are to go with His love, compassion and forgiveness. In Matthew 28 Jesus gives us this charge, "Go out and train everyone you meet, far and near, in this way of life, marking them by baptism in the threefold name: Father, Son, and Holy Spirit. Then instruct them in the practice of all I have commanded you. I'll be with you as you do this, day after day after day, right up to the end of the age." Jesus has handed over his ministry to us as his body. Let us GO! Touch those who suffer from the disease of being unwanted. Let us be The Body of Christ.

Today's Closer Walk

Scripture(s)

For the one whom God has sent speaks the words of God, for God gives the Spirit without limit. John 3:34

Down the Path

Sure Footing

The spirit of the Lord Jesus is in us and he wants to touch a world that suffers from the disease of being unwanted through us. It is our job to touch those whose life needs to be restored or even pieced together. We are the friends of Christ!

Solid Ground

Our response to his call is; Here I am Lord, send me! One by one each of us will make a difference in the lives of those around us. Let's put an end to the disease of being unwanted!

Talking with Jesus

Prayer

Lord Jesus, help me to see those around me that need your touch. Help me to touch and love with your great love.

What are your thoughts as you choose a closer walk with Jesus?

THE MIGHTY OAK

In my daily journey, I often pass a majestic oak tree standing alone in a pasture. I have often admired this oak. It is at least 100 feet tall and almost as wide. This mighty oak is at least 12 to 15 feet in diameter. I sometimes see a herd of cattle resting peacefully in its shade in the heat of the day. I have frequently wondered the age of this impressive oak tree. I have conducted some research on determining the age of trees. I found that measuring the circumference of a tree to determine its age is a guess at best. Experts say that oaks with similar measurements that have been cut down and measured are estimated to be 250 to 300 years old. What a story this oak could tell. This oak has been through many diverse and difficult seasons in its life. This tree has seen harsh summers of drought, fierce windstorms, the threat of lightning, too much rain, bitter cold winters, tornados and hurricanes. In my research, I have learned that in times of drought a tree pushes its roots down deeper in the earth to seek the nourishment and moisture it needs. This tree knows where to find what it needs. In times of drought or difficult circumstances in our spiritual life we need to learn from this oak tree. We need to push through and press on into God, for in Him is all that what we need. Psalm 42:1 says, "As the deer pants for the water brooks, so my soul pants for You, O God. My soul thirsts for God, for the living God." Our thirst and longing for God will cause us to press into God. For it is in God that we know our soul will be satisfied. Psalm 63: 5 says, "My soul shall be satisfied as with the richest food. My mouth shall praise you with joyful lips." In Matthew 11:28 Jesus has the answer for our soul in times of drought: "Are you tired? Worn out? Burned out on religion? Come to me. Get away with me and you'll recover your life. I'll show you how to take a real rest. Walk with me and work with me, watch how I do it. Learn the unforced rhythms of grace. I won't lay anything heavy or ill fitting on you. Keep Company with me and you'll learn to live freely and lightly." Jesus is not only willing, but invites us, to come to him.
It is Jesus, The God of all Comfort, Who makes this invitation. He invites us to come to Him. Jesus is the lover of our souls. His call is to us, His children, who "labor and are heavy laden" in a season of thirst and drought. He cares for us.

He will satisfy each soul. When we come to Jesus, each will be "like a tree planted by streams of water, which yields its fruit in season and whose leaf does not wither." Jeremiah 17:8 says we will be like trees replanted in Eden, putting down roots near the rivers, never a worry through the hottest of summers, never dropping a leaf, serene and calm through droughts, bearing fresh fruit every season. To each I say: Recover your life; find rest for your weary and thirsty soul. Press in and press on into God. Learn from the mighty oak.

Today's Closer Walk

Scripture(s)

The good man will be like a tall tree in his strength; his growth will be as the wide-stretching trees of Lebanon. Psalm 92:12

Down the Path

Sure Footing

We at times will only find what we need in Christ by pushing deeper in fellowship with him. Jesus is what we need. He alone in the one that will satisfy our drought ridden soul. In him is all we need!

Solid Ground

Get away with Jesus and recover your life! Let Jesus show you how to rest in him. He wants fellowship with you more than you could ever imagine. He will show you how to take real rest! Spend time with him today!

Talking with Jesus

Prayer

Lord Jesus, I accept your invitation to come to you with all the burdens of life. I want to live like you, freely and lightly!

What are your thoughts as you choose a closer walk with Jesus?

THE PLAN (PART ONE)

After wandering in the desert for 40 years, it was time for the wonderful plan of God to unfold; it was time for the children of Israel to enter the Promised Land. After the death of Moses, Joshua was now the man of God that would lead this mighty nation. The Lord spoke to Joshua and said, "Arise, and cross the river Jordan in to the land that I will give you." God gave Joshua instructions for entering the Promised Land. God gave him the first step. The plan of God unfolds one step at a time. In addition to the plan, God assured Joshua that he would be with him every step of the way. In Joshua 1:5 God said, "As I was with Moses, so I will be with you; I will never leave you nor forsake you." Joshua was going to see and walk out the plan of God for his life. He was to lead God's people with the assurance that God was with them. God knew that Joshua would face many challenges in walking out the plan for his life. God continues to encourage Joshua. In Joshua 1:6-9, God commands Joshua to be strong and courageous. Three times God repeats this specific command: be courageous. In our walk with God, we will face situations and circumstances that we will not understand. The command from God is to simply be strong, courageous, and not troubled. We have assurance like Joshua. God will be with us every step of the way no matter what we may face. We will face many difficult situations in life. We may find ourselves walking through "the valley of the shadow of death" but we have this promise: God will never leave us nor forsake us. Hebrews 13:5, from the Amplified Bible, puts it this way: "He [God] Himself has said, I will not in any way fail you nor give you up nor leave you without support. **[I will]** not, **[I will]** not, **[I will]** not in any degree leave you helpless nor forsake nor let [you] down (relax My hold on you)! [Assuredly not!]" When God says, "I will not," you can rest assured that **he won't!** Just as God was with Joshua, God will be with us, every step of the way and in each moment of our walk with him. Be courageous! The plan of God is about to unfold.

Today's Closer Walk

Scripture(s)

The Lord is the one who goes ahead of you; He will be with you. He will not fail you or forsake you. Do not fear or be dismayed. Deuteronomy 31:8

Down the Path

Sure Footing

Realize that the plan of God will be revealed one step at a time. God may give you a "big picture" but his plan comes to us in order; divine order. Remember: we walk by faith!

Solid Ground

How do we respond to the plan of God? Be strong; rely on what God has put in our hearts. BE courageous, don't let the fear of what may lie ahead stop you from following each step of his plan for your life.

Talking with Jesus

Prayer

Lord Jesus, I will follow your plan for my life with strength and courage as you command. I trust you! Keep me focused on your great love for me.

What are your thoughts as you choose a closer walk with Jesus?

DAY 23

THE PLAN (PART TWO)

The plan of God was for Joshua and the children of Israel to cross the River Jordan and enter the Promised Land. This would prove to be a great challenge for Joshua. It was spring and the river Jordan was at flood stage. We often wonder why God would lead us in similar ways. Why would God choose this time, at this moment, to lead a great multitude of people across the flood stage waters of the Jordan River? Why would God allow us to go through and face the things we face in our walk with Him? Why would God allow us to face a physical challenge or a financial challenge? Our responsibility to God is to trust Him even though we do not fully understand His direction. Hebrews 10:38 says, "Now the just shall live by faith." Our trust should be in God, who gives the plan, and not in our own understanding. Remember God's ways are different from ours. Isaiah 55:8 says, "For my thoughts are not your thoughts, **neither are your ways my ways,** saith the Lord." Joshua brought the children of Israel to the Jordan River, where they camped before crossing over. This is a great example for us. Joshua knew he had to cross the swollen river. He knew he had a great challenge before him. Joshua knew he could not rush the plan of God, so Joshua waited on God for the details. When God gives us a plan, it is wise to wait on Him for the details. Finally, the Lord gave Joshua the plan. Joshua 3:7-8: "Today I will begin to exalt you in the eyes of all Israel, so they may know that I am with you as I was with Moses. Tell the priests who carry the Ark of the Covenant, 'When you reach the edge of the Jordan's waters, go and stand in the river." Verse 15 continues: "As soon as the priests who carried the ark reached the Jordan and their feet touched the water's edge, the water from upstream stopped flowing. It piled up in a heap a great distance away." The children of Israel walked across the Jordan River on dry ground into the Promised Land. No matter what we may face, God is with us. He will never leave us nor forsake us. He will reveal his plan for us one step at a time, and when He does, He will lead us every step of the way.

When we Trust God completely and wait on Him to work out the details of our lives, we can rest in the comfort that God will bring great blessings to our lives. Our understanding will not always grasp what God is doing in our lives, but we know by faith that God is working out things for our best.

Today's Closer Walk

Scripture(s)

Pile your troubles on God's shoulders, he'll carry your load, he'll help you out. He'll never let good people topple into ruin. Psalm 55:22

Down the Path

Sure Footing

Our trust should be in God, not our understanding. God does not always work in the way we think he should. Sometimes the plan of God makes no "human sense," but when his plan comes together it makes perfect sense!

Solid Ground

In every step, in every way, every day; lean on God! Through deeper fellowship with Jesus we will come to trust him more and more and when we face uncertain situations in the future we can say; I trusted in Jesus before, I'll trust him now! I will have victory.

Talking with Jesus

Prayer

Lord Jesus, draw me closer to you! I thank you that you always have the perfect plan for my life today and everyday! Help me to remember to rest in you and your care for my life.

What are your thoughts as you choose a closer walk with Jesus?

THE UNIVERSITY OF TEMPTATION

Temptation sometimes leads us to things that will separate us from God. James 1:14 says, "When a man is tempted, it is his own passions that carry him away and serve as bait." Temptation is the desire to have or do something that one knows should be avoided. The question is how are we, as followers of Christ, supposed to handle temptation? We need to realize that temptation comes in many forms, shapes, sizes, and for many reasons. None are exempt from temptation. For if Christ was tempted, so will we, as His children, be tempted. We also must recognize that temptation comes again and again. We do not graduate from The University of Temptation. It is a university that we constantly attend and where we are constantly learning. Temptations usually target our weaknesses in the flesh or they appeal to our egos. Jesus was tempted by Satan to turn stones into bread. Satan appealed to Jesus' flesh. Jesus was hungry and Satan saw what he thought was a weakness. He tried to make the most of it. Jesus, as our example, overcame this temptation by standing on the word of God. He said, "Man shall not live by bread alone, but by every word that proceeds from the mouth of God." (Matthew 4) Standing on the word is our first course of action when we face temptation. We also need to understand that we face temptation for many reasons. One reason temptation comes is to **prove** us. I Peter 4:12 tells us: "Beloved, think it not strange concerning the fiery trial among you, which cometh upon you to **prove** you, as though a strange thing happened unto you." Temptation sometimes serves as a spiritual refining process, teaching us where our true strength lies and how to stay strong. Other reasons temptations come are to purge us or to make us stronger or to move us away from things that keep us from deeper fellowship with God. Malachi 3:3 says, "The LORD will **purify** the descendants of Levi, as though they were gold or silver." Spiritual refining is always in motion.

When we face temptations, we need to recognize:
1. **We are not alone**
2. **God will not allow you to be tempted beyond what you can face.**
3. **God will provide the way of escape or the way for you to resist falling into sin through temptation.** 1 Cor. 10:13 says, "No test or temptation that comes your way is beyond the course of what others have had to face." You need to remember that God will never let you down; He will never let you be pushed past your limit; He will always be there to help you go through. Jesus said, "Watch and pray, that ye enter not into temptation: the spirit indeed is ready, but the flesh weak." Matthew 26:41 says, "Stand strong! Stand on the Word of God and fall not!"

Today's Closer Walk

Scripture(s)

The Lord knoweth how to deliver the godly out of temptations, and to reserve the unjust unto the day of judgment to be punished: 2 Peter 2:9

Down the Path

Sure Footing

Temptations is Satan's way of stealing the fellowship you have with God. The goal of the Tempter is to separate you from Jesus and render you useless. Satan will use our own passions to lure us into sin.

Solid Ground

When faced with temptation remember; God will not allow you to be tempted beyond what you can face. Look for God's promise, God said he will provide a way of escape. The closer you are to God the quicker you will realize the escape plan. Stay close to God!

Talking with Jesus

Prayer

Dear Jesus, lead me not into temptation but deliver me from evil. For I love you more than the sin I will enter if I fall into temptation.

What are your thoughts as you choose a closer walk with Jesus?

DAY 25

AN ANSWER FOR THE STRUGGLE

The words in the song by the Imperials, *Praise The Lord,* sums up how we as Christians sometimes feel when we face the struggles of life. This song provides a great answer for us as we struggle through situations that crop up out of nowhere. The answer we find in this song is not just a band-aid; it is a solution that puts the enemy of our faith on the run and teaches us what to do when faced with similar situations. The first verse of the song says, *"When you're up against a struggle that shatters all your dreams, and your hope has been cruelly crushed by Satan's manifesting scheme, and you feel the urge within you to submit to earthly fears don't let the faith you're standing in, seem to disappear."* When the enemy of our faith comes to steal from us, we need to turn to God. We find a great example of a King who found himself in a literal battle, of Satan's manifesting scheme, that seemed hopeless. In Second Chronicles chapter 20, Israel's King Jehoshaphat received an urgent report of an approaching army. A great multitude was coming against Israel. The enemy's army was closing in fast. Jehoshaphat reacted like many of us; he was gripped with fear. However, Jehoshaphat did not submit to his earthly fears. He set himself to seek the Lord. When we are faced with a great trial which tests our faith, our first reaction should be to seek the Lord. God will never be overwhelmed or taken by surprise. The Lord will give us what we need to face what lies ahead. Jehoshaphat prayed, He asked for God's protection. The Lord heard the prayer of Jehoshaphat and said, "Do not fear or be dismayed because of this great multitude, for the battle is not yours, but God's. You need not fight in this battle, the LORD is with you." How awesome to hear from God in our time of need. God was going to fight for his people. Jehoshaphat was strengthened and encouraged. God removed Jehoshaphat's fear. Jehoshaphat was so encouraged that he appointed those who sang to the LORD and those who praised the Lord to go out before the army.

Jehoshaphat sent the praise team before the army. Jehoshaphat sealed the deliverance of his people with praise. This is our answer when our faith is tested! Seek the Lord and Praise him for the victory. Praise is what puts the enemy on the run. God inhabits the praise of His people and He works on our behalf. He fights for us! The second verse of the song by the Imperials says it best, *"Praise the Lord He can work with those who praise Him, Praise the Lord, For our God inhabits praise, Praise the Lord, For the chains that seem to bind you Serve only to remind you that they drop powerless behind you When you praise him."* When the battle against Israel started, God set ambushes against the enemy. The great multitude fought each other. When the battle was over, no one in the enemy's army had escaped. Israel's enemies were totally destroyed. God fought for his people. Know that God will fight for you. Praise Him!

Today's Closer Walk

Scripture(s)

But thou [art] holy, [O thou] that inhabitest the praises of Israel. Psalm 22:3

Down the Path

Sure Footing

No matter what road block Satan tries to put in our way, we do not have to submit to earthly fears. We serve a heavenly God. He has all the heavenly answers we need. Realize that we are more than conqueror. God fights for US!

Solid Ground

It's never wrong to praise the Lord! When struggles come our way; Praise Jesus for his mighty delivering power. Praise him for victory. God inhabits your praise. Sing his praises loud and sing his praises long for God is awesome!

Talking with Jesus

Prayer

Thank you Lord that I can lift my voice in praise to you anytime and anywhere. Help me to glorify you through the praise I sing to you.

What are your thoughts as you choose a closer walk with Jesus?

DAY 26

WHO ARE YOU

While making a deposit at my bank, I noticed Ann, a teller that usually works at the downtown branch. I was at the downtown branch the day before and saw Ann there. I made the comment that she must be a twin because she seemed to be at every branch of the bank. Ann said, "Oh no, this world doesn't need two of me." Ann said this in a negative way about herself and I knew Ann was a Christian. I felt like Ann needed an encouraging word. I said, "Ann, you are what God says you are." "You are the light of the world. You are the salt of the earth; People need what God has inside of you". The heaviness seemed to melt from Ann's face and she said, "You're right, I have had a stressful day and sometimes I lose sight of what is real."

In our walk with Jesus, it is easy to lose sight of what is important. It is easy to look at our lives and see no value. It is easy to have a dim view of who we are. The truth is that we are who God says we are. As followers of Christ, we are not what or whom the world says we are. We are not whom our families say we are. We are not whom Satan says we are. As Christians, we live by the word of God, not the word of the world.

Here are just a few things that God says about who we are in Christ: We are the light of the world. We are here to be light, bringing out the God-colors in the world. (Matthew 5:14) We are the salt of the earth. We are here to be salt-seasoning that brings out the God-flavors of this earth. If we lose our saltiness, how will people taste godliness? If we have a sour view of ourselves, how will people come to know Jesus through us? (Matthew 5:13) We are the righteousness of God in Christ Jesus. When God looks at us He sees people who are in right standing with Him through Jesus. (2 Corinthians 5:21)

We are a Royal Priesthood, a holy nation, a chosen generation. We are the ones chosen by God. We are God's instruments to do His work and speak out for Him, to tell others of the night-and-day difference He made for us, from nothing to something, from rejected to accepted. We are a chosen race, a royal priesthood, a dedicated nation; [God's] own purchased, special people, that we may set forth the wonderful deeds and display the virtues and perfections of Him Who called us out of darkness into His marvelous light. (I Peter 2:9) We are healed. He sent his word and made them well. (Psalm 107:20) We are forgiven. (1 John 1:9) **We are who God says we are!**

Today's Closer Walk

Scripture(s)

But you are a chosen people, a royal priesthood, a holy nation, a people belonging to God, that you may declare the praises of him who called you out of darkness into his wonderful light. I Peter 2:9

Down the Path

Sure Footing

You are who God says you are! You are not what the world thinks you are. You are not what you think you are. It is God who declares you to be his righteousness, his royal priesthood and the salt of the earth!

Solid Ground

Thank God that you don't have to wear the titles the world may give you. Walk in what he is called you to be! This world needs salt and light and that is what you are!

Talking with Jesus

Prayer

Dear Jesus, help me to remember my rightful place in you. Help me to walk as salt and light. Jesus, shine through me. Provide spice to those you would have me touch through you.

What are your thoughts as you choose a closer walk with Jesus?

SEAL PUPS AND SHEEP

Sub Antarctic fur seal mothers leave their pups while they are still young, too young to fend for themselves to make long and frequent feeding trips out to sea. When the mothers return from the ocean with provisions for her young, she has to find her young pup among several hundred other seal babies that look alike and act alike. Momma seal is not on a random search; she wants and finds her baby. Momma seal can easily find and recognize her baby and her baby recognizes it's momma. How is this possible?

Jesus said, "My sheep listen to my voice; I know them, and they follow me". How is this possible? How does Jesus know us and care for us? Even the Psalmist asks the question in Psalm 8, "What is man that you are mindful of him, the son of man that you care for him? Mark, a friend of mine expressed it this way, He said, "I feel so significantly insignificant in the eyes of God. I think of all the people in the world, it overwhelms me that God knows me". Not only does God know all about us, he even knows number of hairs on our heads, he desires fellowship with us. Each of us! We can know the voice of our Lord Jesus through intimate daily fellowship with him. Have you ever been in a crowd and heard your name? Out of all the noise and confusion, you hear and recognize the voice of the one calling your name. Chances are that the one calling your name knows you well and in turn you know them just as well. There is a definite connection between the one calling and the one that hears. Jesus said, "My sheep recognize my voice. I know them, and they follow me. I give them real and eternal life". (John 10 MSG) In this world with all the noise and confusion there is the voice of One who calls out to us with a heart of love and un-limited grace with a desire to fellowship with us. God longs for us to recognize his loving voice in every situation. Oftentimes, his voice comes to me like the whisper on the wind.

As we live our daily lives like going to work, doing the most commonplace and mundane tasks, remember this; God is with you every step of the way, When you have to face difficult people, God is with you. The mother seal is programmed by God to know her pup. In contrast, God gives us the choice to fellowship with him, he knows and loves us. His desire for us is that we will choose to spend time with Him daily and in turn we will come to recognize his loving voice.

Today's Closer Walk

Scripture(s)

Yes, Joyful are those who live like this, joyful indeed are those whose God is The Lord. Psalms 144:15

Down the Path

Sure Footing

God is with you every day and in every way. He knows you, you are his child. Listen as he calls your name in a gentle loving way.

Solid Ground

Declare today that you hear God's voice! The noise and confusion of life will not hinder the gentle loving voice of your Heavenly Father.

Talking with Jesus

Prayer

Lord Jesus, my ears are tuned to hear your voice, let us talk together today.

What are your thoughts as you choose a closer walk with Jesus?

WHO DO YOU LOVE?

It is said that if you want to know what or whom a person loves just look where they spend their time and money. I have friends that love NASCAR. They not only love it, they live it as much as good sense will allow. They wear NASCAR tee shirts, hats and belts. They put their favorite driver's number on their own car and sometimes drive around town like they are on the last lap at Talladega. It's not uncommon to hear, "Come here, Jimmy, Dale, Junior, Rusty, or Jeff" as these parents call for their kids. Some pets have even been blessed with these famous names. Some people will go as far as skipping church just to watch a race on Sunday. When we love something or someone, it makes perfect sense to wear a checkered flag tuxedo to your best friend's, Rusty Dale's, wedding and to take your dog Junior with you.

Jesus said "If you love me, show it by doing what I've told you. (John 14:15) Do those around you know what or whom you love? Obedience to our Lord and what He has asked us, and sometimes commands us, to do is the fruit of the love we have for Him. If we love Him, we will willingly follow His lead in the way He lived His life in the Father, and the way He treated others. Do we love our Lord so much so that we are willing to dress ourselves in Him daily so that we reflect His love, compassion, and forgiveness? Romans 13:12 says, "Clothe yourself with the Lord Jesus Christ (the Messiah)." (AMP) Dressing ourselves in Christ is to be in Him and He in us. In this, we are compelled to love Him, for in Him we have salvation. We are covered in his blood and covered by His sacrifice. We are led by His Spirit and we will touch the world as He touched the world because of the great love we have for Him. The love that Jesus had for His Father was evident because He did what His Father asked of Him. Jesus reflected the True and Living God to a world lost in its sin. Do we love Jesus so much so that we would even skip a NASCAR race to go to church?

Today's Closer Walk

Scripture(s)

Pray that you ... may have power, together with all the saints, to grasp how wide and long and high and deep is the love of Christ. Ephesians 3:17-19

Down the Path

Sure Footing

What or whom do you love? It shows in how you spend your time. It has been said, If you want to know what someone loves look at how they spend their time, energy and money. Would those around you know that you love Jesus?

Solid Ground

Take time to reflect on the great love God has given us through Jesus. God took time and spared no expense to show us that he loves us.

Talking with Jesus

Prayer

Lord Jesus, help me to love you more!

What are your thoughts as you choose a closer walk with Jesus?

Who Do You Say That I Am?

In Matthew 16:13-15 Jesus was with his disciples at the coast of Caesarea Philippi. Jesus asked His disciples a very important question: "Whom do men say that I the son of man am?" Why would Jesus ask what other people thought about who He was? Perhaps, Jesus wanted to see what the world perceived Him to be or possibly He wanted to see what message the world was hearing. His disciples answered:"Some say that you are John the Baptist, some say Elijah, or Jeremiah or one of the prophets." If we were to ask the average person who Jesus is, we would get the same type of answer. Some people would say Jesus was a great teacher, a notable prophet, and an important person. We would get a variety of answers from the casual observer of Jesus and His teachings. These observations are made from a world on the outside looking in at the life of Jesus.

Jesus asked the question again but this time He asked the question directly to His disciples. "What about you?" "Who do you say that I am?" Jesus asked this question, not to the world but to those who were intimately connected to Him, his disciples. His disciples were with Jesus night and day. They saw Jesus heal the sick and teach the multitudes. They saw the captives set free. His disciples watched Jesus when He fed the five thousand. They saw the miracles and the compassion of God first hand. They knew Jesus and yet, He asked them, "Who do you say that I am?"

Peter answered, "Thou art the Christ, the son of the living God." Jesus answered and said to Peter, "Blessed art thou, for flesh and blood hath not revealed it unto thee but my Father which is in heaven." Peter answered the question as one who had and was experiencing the True and Living Christ. Peter knew Jesus.

As followers of Jesus today, how do we answer the question, when Jesus asks, "Who do you say that I am?" When we go to work, can others see Jesus in us? Do we declare Him to be the Son of the Living God by the way we live our lives? Can the world see a good man or a good teacher? Can the world in which we live see Christ, the Son of the Living God, living through us? Can the sick count on us to pray for them? Can a lost world count on us to share the Good News of salvation to them? Can those who need compassion count on us? We answer the question everyday by the way we live. Do we live our lives as if we know the son of the Living God? If Jesus were to come to us as His followers and ask, "Who do you say that I am?" Would our lives or our testimony declare Jesus to be the

True and Living God in our lives? Would our walk with the True and Living God answer his question?

Today's Closer Walk

Scripture(s)

Let your light so shine before men, that they may see your good works, and glorify your Father which is in heaven. Matthew 5:16

Down the Path

Sure Footing

The way we live our lives shows the world who Jesus is in our lives. We reflect what we believe by how we act and react to those around us. Can the waiter where you ate lunch today tell that you serve Jesus? Can the driver that cut you off in traffic tell that you are a follower of Christ?

Solid Ground

The world is watching and waiting for hope, peace and Joy in their everyday lives. God wants your life to reflect who he is, He wants to fellowship and reach out to those in your world through you.

Talking with Jesus

Prayer

Lord Jesus, help me to reflect who you are to those around me.

What are your thoughts as you choose a closer walk with Jesus?

DAY **30**

Why Aren't You Celebrating?

In a scene from the movie *A Good Year*, Max, a young man of about 10, is playing his uncle Henry in a tennis match. Uncle Henry lines up his serve. THAWCK! Dead center. Max lunges for the ball as if his life depended on it, but misses. Uncle Henry yells, Ace! Game, Set, match! Uncle Henry gloats without mercy. Max yells out, "You don't have to rub it in." Uncle Henry says, "The real question, Max, is why aren't you celebrating". Young Max answers, "Because I lost." Uncle Henry tells Max, "A man should acknowledge his losses as gracefully as he celebrates his victories. Someday, Max, you'll come to see that a man learns nothing from winning. The act of losing, however can elicit great wisdom." In James chapter 1, James conveys a similar but much more powerful biblical principle. James says, "Consider it wholly joyful, my brethren, whenever you are enveloped in or encounter trials of any sort or fall into various temptations. Be assured and understand that the trial and proving of your faith bring out endurance and steadfastness and patience." Consider it a sheer gift, friends, when tests and challenges come at you from all sides. You know that under pressure, your faith-life is forced into the open and shows its true colors. So don't try to get out of anything prematurely. Let trials of any sort or different temptations do their work so you become mature and well developed, not deficient in any way. What we face in our journey of faith is not to break us but to make us, to prove us. Trials and tests are to show us that we can and must depend on Jesus in every step and in every moment of our faith journey. It is easy to celebrate the good things in life on the mountaintop, however James says, "Celebrate with joy when you are tested, tempted, and tried." Paul, in Romans chapter 5 says, "We continue to shout our praise even when we're hemmed in with troubles, because we know how troubles can develop passionate patience in us, and how that patience in turn forges the tempered steel of virtue, keeping us alert for whatever God will do next." In alert expectancy such as this, we're never left feeling shortchanged.

Quite the contrary, we can't round up enough containers to hold everything God generously pours into our lives through the Holy Spirit! Some things to consider when we are tested. **First:** Know that God has allowed this test for a purpose. Search diligently for God's purpose in every trial you face. **Second:** Thank God that, through this trial or test of our faith, we are becoming more Christ-like in our faith journey and, in turn, will enjoy a closer fellowship with Jesus. **Third:** Tests and trials reflect the strength of character we have. Can we forgive? Can we turn the other cheek as Jesus commands? We learn a lot about ourselves by the trials we face. **Finally:** Thank God for promising to be with you in all you face. Know that you are never alone. God's plan is to bring you into closer fellowship with him. The real question is: "Why aren't we celebrating?"

Today's Closer Walk

Scripture(s)

We can rejoice, too, when we run into problems and trials, for we know that they help us develop endurance. Romans 5:3

Down the Path

Sure Footing

The challenges, tests, bad days, blue moments in life, sometime come to make our faith stronger. It's hard to realize in the moment of what seems to be defeat or in the midst of our faith being tested, but it's true. Test of our faith come to prove us and often times to purge out of things that hold us back in our walk with Jesus.

Solid Ground

When the dust settles and we walk out of the valley of the testing and the trying of our faith, we become stronger in our faith and in turn we will move closer to God.

Talking with Jesus

Prayer

Lord Jesus, help me to find joy when my faith is tested.

What are your thoughts as you choose a closer walk with Jesus?

DAY 31

"I'M GOING TO DO WHAT YOU DO"

One morning while driving my son Anthony to his soccer game he turned to me and said, "Dad, I know what I'm going to do when I grow up, I'm going to do what you do." What Anthony said to me was sobering to say the least. My life as Anthony's father flashed before my eyes. What kind of an example had I been for him? Would he grow up knowing and loving God? Would Anthony be a man of faith and honor? Was I a man worth following? The truth of the matter is: Anthony is going to be a reflection of the life I have shown him. He will learn a great deal about life from the way I live it. He will learn a good deal about walking in faith from me. As parents, we have a huge responsibility when it comes to raising our children. Our job is to raise our sons and daughters to know and love the Lord. Proverbs 22:6 gives us great advice: "Point your kids in the right direction when they're old they won't be lost." I began to think about my own father and the impressions he left on my life when I was young. My dad's job required a lot of time on the road making sales calls. However, he would sometimes drive 500 miles just to watch me play baseball. I knew my dad would always be there. Because of his example of love for me, it was easy for me to believe that my Heavenly Father loved me and would always be there for me. I want Anthony to feel the same way. Thanks Dad! I saw my dad go through tough times in his life. I remember the year he lost his job. Dad never grew discouraged. He never lost heart nor his faith in God. Dad knew that God was working in his behalf to bring blessings to his life and our family. As a result, when I faced tough times in my life, I thought of my father. I did what I saw him do. I trusted God and God has always been faithful to his promises. Thanks Dad! Paul said in 1 Corinthians 11:1, "Be imitators of me, in so far as I in turn am an imitator of Christ." The way we as parents should live should echo the words of the Apostle Paul. The way we speak to our children is by the way we live and deal with life. Our lives as parents should say, "Imitate me; pattern your life after mine; and follow my example."

As parents, we should strive to be men worth following, men of honor, men that teach our children to know God, just like my dad did for me. Our children need to learn to love the Lord from us. They need to know how to treat others. Our kids need to learn how to forgive and give. When tough times come, they need to know whom to trust. It is our job, as parents, to live our lives in such a way that when our kids are old they won't be lost. Will you be pleased if your children say, "Dad, I'm going to do what you do."

Today's Closer Walk

Scripture(s)

Be imitators of me, just as I also am of Christ. Philippians 3:17

Down the Path

Sure Footing

We are being watched and imitated by those we influence the most. What an awesome responsibility this fact imposes on us! Be careful with the influence you have because you are going to see it at work in the future.

Solid Ground

Seek daily to use the influence you have for Gods Glory. Children are God's gift to us. Allow God to show you how to be a Godly influence, so that what you see in the future glorifies Him.

Talking with Jesus

Prayer

Lord Jesus, help me be a person worth imitating.

What are your thoughts as you choose a closer walk with Jesus?

Acknowledgements

Just a Closer Walk with Thee Anonymous/Unknown

Yes, Lord, Yes   by; Lynn Keeseker

Britannica online encyclopedia article on Florence Chadwick

Things people said Yogi Berra Quotes http://www.rinkworks.com/said/yogiberra.shtml

Inside 403rd Wing 53rd Weather Reconnaissance Squadron "Hurricane Hunters" http://www.403wg.afrc.af.mil/index.asp

The Book of Acts and Paul in Roman Custody By Brian Rapske

Mother Teresa Biography - Biography.com www.biography.com/articles/Mother-Teresa-9504160

WikiAnswers - How do you estimate the age of an oak tree wiki.answers.com/.../How_do_you_estimate_the_age_of_an_oak_tree –

Jesus, Lover of My Soul By Charles Wesley

Praise The Lord By The Imperials

A Good Year Source Material (from novel: "A Good Year") By Peter Mayle 20th Century Fox Distribution, 20th Century Fox International Scott Free Productions

JUST A CLOSER WALK

A young man was once asked by his friends how he knew he was saved. The young man thought for a while, then said, "you know how it is when you go fishing and catch a fish, you can't see the fish, you only feel the fish tugging on the line. That's how it was when I got saved. I just felt God tugging on my heart.

My hope is that as you read and interact with these daily devotions for the next 31 days, is that God will tug on your heart in a gentle loving way and that you will realize just how much you are loved and cherished by your Heavenly Father.

Printed in the United States
By Bookmasters